Upward Path

A 30-Day Devotional
for Spiritual Training

By
Lori Price

Upward Path for Spiritual Training

Table of Contents

Day 1
Relinquish Control

The plans of the heart belong to man, but the answer of the tongue is from Yahweh. Proverbs 16:1 (WEB)

I sat dumbfounded at my desk. The day was not going exactly how I wanted it to, and now this…. the computer decided to lose the internet connection. I tried everything that I could think of to fix the problem, but my best efforts failed. I gave up trying to solve the problem, and in my desperation, I called technical support for help. A few minutes later a dialog box appeared on the screen with the question: "May I have permission to access your computer remotely?" I quickly answered "yes!" As I sat helplessly by, I watched the computer screen in amazement as the master controller took over. The mouse moved across the screen at a quick pace - click, click, click done. Just like that, he fixed it! He only needed my permission to gain access and take over control. My decision to relinquish control over to the computer master had solved the problem!

The Bible gives an account of a man humbly kneeling before Jesus asking Him to heal his son who was ill. Mathew 17 tells us that the boy's father brought his son to the disciples in hopes his son would be healed, however the disciples could not heal him. We don't know what method the disciples used, but whatever it was, their best efforts had failed, and they could not heal the boy on their own. In desperation, the boy's father relinquishes control over to the Master, Jesus and at that moment, the boy was immediately healed. What the disciples could not do, Jesus did. Amazing things happen when we relinquish control to Jesus!

When we realize that we cannot change our circumstances on our own, and we turn over our struggles, anxiety, and worries to the Lord, that is when He can begin to heal our lives. What are you hanging onto in life that you think you can fix on your own? Is it your finances? Is it a broken marriage? Is it an addictive habit that you are too ashamed to admit you have? God wants to help you. He wants to fix it for you. He wants your permission to gain access into that area before He will fix it. He is waiting for you to relinquish control to Him!

Heavenly Father, help us to realize that the problems in our life are too big for us to handle alone. Help us swallow our pride and reach out to You with a humble heart knowing that You are the Master Controller just standing by waiting to take over and heal us. Amen!

ADDITIONAL READING

1 Peter 5:7   **Hebrews 4:16**   **Isaiah 41:10**

Day 1: Questions to Ponder

1) What area in life are you struggling with that is out of control?

2) What is keeping you from "relinquishing control" to God?

3) Will you give the "Master Controller" permission to access that troubled area in your life?

Day 1 Journal Notes

Day 2
Heavy Load

To the chief Musician for the sons of Korah, A Song upon Alamoth.
God is our refuge and strength, a very present help in trouble.
Psalm 46:1(KJV)

One of my favorite exercises in the gym is the bench press. It's like a 3 for 1 deal! It works your triceps, shoulders, and chest but I don't like doing it alone. My fear is that once I bring it down to the chest, and the load is too heavy, I may not be able to push it back up. That is where my friend and workout partner comes in. She is my spotter. (a spotter keeps watch on the weightlifter making sure the exercise is done correctly) She closely watches, making sure my form is correct. When she sees me begin to struggle, she moves in close letting me know she is there if I need her. Her encouragement to do one more repetition pushes me past what I thought I could do. As my arms begin to shake, she will place her hands under the bar making sure I don't drop it and as my muscles begin to fatigue and I can no longer bear the load, she pulls up on the bar removing the heavy load.

Our heavenly Father is always present in times of trouble. When we are in the middle of a trial, we may think we are alone, but we are not. God is always present. In Isaiah 43:2 we are reminded that God is with us in every situation, every storm we may go through, and every trial that comes our way. God's Word promises that He will be with us through the difficult times and through our struggles. He keeps watch over us every moment of our life. He sees us under a heavy load, or a stressful situation. He sees our faith begin to shake. He moves in close, ready to help in times of trouble, (Psalms 46:1); He knows the right time to place His hands around the "bar" and remove the "heavy load" if it becomes too much. God is our deliverer and our refuge in times of trouble. He loves us, will never fail us, and He is always there to help us; all we must do is ask Him. When the heavy load of this world begins to weigh you down, and anxiety, depression, or fear begin to overcome you, call upon the Lord for help. He will move in close, wrap His arms of comfort around you, and be your ever-present help in times of trouble. Let Him be your refuge, hiding place, and sanctuary when you need a place to rest.

Father, I pray that in times of stress and trouble, that You would remind us that You are there watching and that You see us. Remind us that when the load gets too heavy, that it is You who will step in and bring us through it. Amen!

ADDITIONAL READING

Psalms 121:1-2   **Nahum 1:7**   **Psalms 18:2**

Day 2: Questions to Ponder

1. What heavy load or stressful situation are you carrying around in life?

2. Do you see God as your "spotter" ready to help in times of need?

3. What area of your life do you need God's help to remove or carry the heavy load?

Day 2 Journal Notes

Day 3
Perfect Timing

To everything there is a season, and a time to every purpose under the heaven: Ecclesiastes 3:1(WEB)

Tess was sitting on her sofa at 1:30 am watching television. She couldn't sleep so she turned on the T.V. for a late-night show. She was under stress since she had been the sole caretaker of her aunt who was bedridden. I sat and listened intently as she told me what happened next. A car traveling at a high rate of speed had lost control, took out two trees and a fence before reaching her house. As it slammed into her living room, the car hit the sofa she was sitting on, sending her flying across the room. Tess was a little banged up, but thankfully, no broken bones. After looking at the damaged house which was recently boarded, I was amazed that Tess survived this ordeal. She looked at me and said "It wasn't my time to go yet!". She credited God for having His protective hand on her. God decided it was not her time to leave this earth.

The story of Esther is one example of God's impeccable timing. Esther was appointed queen at a time when her people, the Jews, were under persecution. Her uncle, Mordechai, hears of the plot to exterminate all the Jews. He sends word to the queen urging her to petition the King and stop this from happening. As was the custom of that day, anyone approaching the King without being summoned could be killed. Esther was terrified knowing very well her life could be taken. After all, catch a King at a bad time and it could mean sudden death for you, so who wouldn't be afraid. However, Mordechai doesn't take no for an answer and tells her that maybe she was appointed queen for a time like this (Esther 4:1). The words Mordechai spoke penetrated her heart, and she agreed to approach the king. After much prayer and fasting, she enters the courts of the King. As she approached, he held out his scepter, which meant he accepted her, and that her life would be spared. He not only spares her life but grants her anything she wants. And with that, she makes known to the king the evil plot to exterminate her people. The

King immediately puts a halt to the evil plot and the very one that sought to kill the Jewish people was the one who was killed.

God's timing is always perfect. If we allow it, even the words we speak can be used of God at that perfect time. Proverbs 25:11 reminds us of words timely spoken are like apples of gold. Esther was placed in the right position at the perfect time and entered the Kings court with her request in God's timing, to bring about God's perfect will.

When things don't seem to come together according to your time frame, just remember, our timing is not always God's timing, but God's timing is ALWAYS the right timing!

Father God, help us to be sensitive to your leading. When things don't work out according to our time clock, help us to remember that You are working out all things in your perfect timing. Amen!

ADDITIONAL READING

Proverbs 25:11   **Galatians 6:9**   **Ecclesiastes 3:11**

Day 3: Questions to Ponder

1) Is waiting on God's timing difficult for you?

2) Name a time when God answered a prayer that you thought was at the last minute.

3) What words of encouragement have you spoken to someone while they were waiting on God to answer their prayer?

Day 3 Journal Notes

Day 4
Curveballs

For I know the thoughts that I think toward you, says Yahweh, thoughts of peace, and not of evil, to give you hope and a future.
Jeremiah 29:11(WEB)

A curve ball is one of the most effective ways to strike out a batter. The batter sees the pitch coming straight at him and he plans his hit. All of sudden just before reaching the plate, the ball drops, and changes course, either inward or outward, which throws the batter off balance. The batter hangs his head in defeat as he hears the word "STRIKE"!

This morning, I arrived at the gym at my usual time, only to find it closed. It was an unexpected interruption (or as I like to call it, a curve ball) of my day and it frustrated me. I like to plan my day and when things don't go the way I plan, it throws me off balance.

The story of Joseph is found in Genesis 29 and tells us of his experience with a curve ball. Joseph was his father's favorite son and he was hated by his brothers. One day, his father sent him out to the field to check on his brothers. Filled with jealousy and seeing the opportunity to get rid of Joseph, his brothers overtook him and sold him into slavery. I'm sure Joseph thought it was going to be a normal day when he took a walk through the field, but life is not always normal. Sometimes we go along the journey of life, planning our ways, not expecting changes to happen, or at least not the changes we didn't plan for, when suddenly here comes a curve ball that knocks us off balance. It could be a pipe that breaks and floods our house right before a planned celebration; it could be the company we work for that goes bankrupt, or the doctor report that comes back with a less than desirable outcome. We may begin to question God, thinking if He really loves us, then why did He let this happen? But God ALWAYS has a bigger plan. If we look past the event that has thrown us off balance, and trust that God is at work even through our "unexpected interruption", we will see Him at work. It is through these events that our faith in the Lord has an opportunity to grow. If we never became sick, we would not experience His healing power and if we never struggled financially, we would never experience His providing hand.

Joseph's story did not end after being sold into slavery. After a series of unexpected interruptions, his patience and choice to trust the Lord paid off. He eventually becomes governor over Egypt, saving the nation from a severe famine. So, when you are thrown a curve ball remember, it is God who allowed it and there is always a reason for it!

Father God, as we walk through life and experience difficulty, remind us it is You who has allowed our unexpected interruptions. May our faith in You grow stronger and may we choose to trust that You are in control of all that we encounter. Amen!

ADDITIONAL READING

Proverbs 19:21   **Isaiah 55:8-9**   **Psalm 138:8**

Day 4: Questions to Ponder

1) Do you become frustrated when the day you have planned suddenly changes due to unforeseen events?

2) Name a time when you made plans for something special only to have a curveball or unexpected interruption change those plans.

3) What unexpected interruption is occurring in your life that God could be using to get your attention?

Day 4 Journal Notes

Day 5
365 Days of Thanksgiving

Enter into his gates with thanksgiving, and into his courts with praise: be thankful unto him, and bless his name. Psalm 100:4(KJV)

Once a year we celebrate being thankful. It is called Thanksgiving. It's a time of year most people like to express why they are thankful. Everyone has something to be thankful for. Being thankful for all that God has given to me is something I am trying to express every day, and it is good practice. It takes our focus off what we don't have and places it on all that we do have. I am thankful for many things in my life. For one, the love and acceptance God shows me and for giving His own Son to take my place on the cross. I am thankful that God has blessed me with a mother who continually prays for me and always has an encouraging word to say. I am thankful that God sent me a faithful friend and workout partner, Cyndi, who has made me stronger physically and continues to encourage me in my walk with the Lord.

In the book of Luke, it tells the story of a man who had two sons. The youngest son demands his inheritance and after receiving it, leaves home. He spends the money on women and whiskey. With no money left, he begins to realize what a fool he has been and begins his journey back home to his father, hoping his father will at least give him a job as a servant. As he approaches home, his father sees him coming back home and is filled with compassion for his son and excited that he has returned home. His father orders a feast to celebrate his return. This once lost son who had left his father's house to seek his own selfish desires had returned home. I'm sure that was something the father continued to give thanks for on a daily basis!

Sometimes in our prayers, we tend to point out to God what we don't have; but even in our prayers we are encouraged to give thanks. In Philippians we are reminded to not worry about anything, but rather to pray about what is causing us to be anxious. This verse is a constant reminder to me to continue giving thanks to God even when I am in the middle of a difficult trial.

This Thanksgiving begin a daily practice of giving thanks to God for at least one thing. If you do, this time next year, you will have given Him 365 days of Thanksgiving!

Father, thank You for all You have given us in life. Help us to remember all You have done for us. May we give You thanks on a daily basis and not grumble about what we don't have. Help turn our focus on all of the blessings You have given us and teach us to praise You and to give You thanks. Amen!

ADDITIONAL READING

Ephesians 5:20   Psalm 95:2   Matthew 15:36

Day 5: Questions to Ponder

1) What are your most thankful for?

2) Has anyone ever thanked you for a job well done?

3) Do you thank God in the midst of a trial or only when something good happens?

Day 5 Journal Notes

Day 6
Pruning

I am the true vine, and my Father is the farmer. Every branch in me that doesn't bear fruit, he takes away. Every branch that bears fruit, he prunes, that it may bear more fruit. John 15:1-2(WEB)

I'm not good at growing things, so I never paid much attention to the plant growing on my patio. That is until my friend gave me a succulent. In one of her creative moments, she began putting together these beautiful succulents in pots which I grew to admire. She has a green thumb and is quite creative. I took the succulent she gave me home, watered it, placed it in sunlight, and it still looks beautiful!

The plant on my back patio was there when I moved in. I had no idea what it was. It grew quickly, took up space, and blocked my satellite dish. I didn't see much value in it, so a few months ago, I decided to trim it back. I began cutting it back, leaf by leaf and I cut the trunk very low, but it sprouted back up just a few months later bringing with it friends; two additional plants growing right next to it. What happened next surprised me. I noticed these green, half-moon shaped objects growing on the tree. It began to bear fruit. Bananas! It turned out to be a dwarf banana tree. In all actuality, I had no idea what I was doing when I cut it back (remember, I'm the one that can't grow things), but this once annoying plant, soon became the center of my attention, and now I find myself making sure it gets the care it needs. I don't know who planted it originally, but I'm glad I get to enjoy the fruit!

Pruning in our lives is a necessary step if you want to see fruit of any kind. It can be painful, but the result is well worth it. The apostle John speaks about this in John 15 where he teaches us that God is the gardener, and that God prunes us so we can bear more fruit. The Greek word for "prune" (Katharos) literally means to cleanse or purge by removing undesirable elements. Anything that would harm you or gets in the way of your growth with God could be considered an "undesirable element". When we are going through the pruning process, and God begins to remove those "undesirable elements" within us, He is doing it so that more of His fruit can grow within us. His fruit includes: love, joy, peace, patience, kindness, goodness, humility, and self-control. (Galatians 5:22). These fruits are what God has intended for us so we can reflect more of His image in our lives.

Just as the banana tree on my back patio is now growing fruit, if we abide in Christ, and allow Him to prune us and remove things that hinder our walk with Him, we will begin to see His fruit in our lives.

Father, may we be willing to allow You to remove all our character defects, in our life that gets in the way of bearing fruit. As we begin to feel the pain of pruning, wrap Your arms of comfort around us and gently remind us that You are with us, and the end result will be well worth it. Amen!

ADDITIONAL READING

John 15:8   Matthew 7:16-17   Psalm 1:3

Day 6: Questions to Ponder

1) What area of your life needs pruning?

2) Is there an undesirable element that God is trying to remove from your life in order to reflect more of His image in your life?

3) Which "fruit of the Spirit" do you need God to help grow in your life?

Day 6 Journal Notes

Day 7
The Irritant & the Pearl

Count it all joy, my brothers, when you fall into various temptations,
knowing that the testing of your faith produces endurance.
James 1:2-3(WEB)

In 2008, a couple in Florida stopped to have a clam dinner at a seafood restaurant. After biting down on something hard, they discovered it was a pearl. Experts say, it is rare to find a pearl in a clam, since pearls are usually found in oysters, but it happens, and when it does, your reward can be great! (if you don't break your teeth in the process). What I find intriguing is the process in which the pearl is formed. During the feeding process, small particles called irritants, (I like to call them intruders or unwanted guests) enter the clam, and contribute to forming the pearl. The clam responds to the intruder by secreting fluid which coats the unwanted guest. The final product: a pearl. Without the irritating intruders, there would be no pearl!

We all have some form of irritants in our life. For some, it's the people at our job; the irritating co-worker that gossips about you then asks you to pray for her when she is troubled; the guy that just cut you off on the freeway because he wanted your lane; or the annoying neighbor that suddenly appears at your door wanting to chat non-stop when you don't have the time.

In the above passage, James reminds us to remain steadfast when going through trials, because in the end we will be complete lacking nothing. The trials we experience are part of the process. I believe God uses trials or irritating people that we come in contact with to help cultivate us into a "Pearl". When we encounter trials or what we may call irritating moments, we can choose to endure the process and recognize that God allowed it to help form us into His image, complete, lacking nothing.

Oh, and let's not forget, sometimes we are the irritant in others' lives. I know I can be, just ask my family. I take great joy in knowing that I helped in the process of forming their "Pearl"!

Father, our lives are filled with challenging moments and sometimes the people we encounter can be difficult to love. In those times, remind us that You are using all circumstances to help change us and form us into Your image...complete...lacking nothing. Amen!

ADDITIONAL READING

1 Peter 4:12-13　　　**James 1:12**　　　**John 16:33**

Day 7: Questions to Ponder

1) When trials come into your life, do you greet them with joy or are you surprised God allowed them?

2) Has God allowed an "intruder" or "irritating person" in your life that you are praying for?

3) What area of your life is God testing to form a "Pearl"?

Day 7 Journal Notes

Day 8
What's in a Name

I will praise thee; for I am fearfully and wonderfully made; Marvelous are thy works; and that my soul knoweth right well. Psalm 139:14(KJV)

People often label others as they see them which can be especially devastating to a child. Growing up, I was teased and called "freckle face". I had so many freckles, you could play "connect the dots" with them! I remember feeling hurt by this name; However, my mama called them "Angel kisses". I liked that definition better!

This past week, I listened to my friend, Cindy, teach on names and labels that people place on us or we give to ourselves. During the teaching, she gave us an exercise. She passed out name tags. First, we were to write on a piece of paper what "name" others had given us or what we "labeled" ourselves. Next, we crossed off those negative beliefs or labels we had about ourselves and asked: "What does God think of me?" Then, we were to write on the name tag what God has changed our label to. It was quite inspiring to hear her insight. This once "shy and timid" individual who never saw herself as someone who could ever speak in front of a crowd was now teaching in boldness and confidence! God had changed her label to how He created her. No longer shy, fearful, or timid; she was now bold, confident, and speaking God's word of freedom and healing in front of a crowd! She was living out God's word as it says: "God has not given us the spirit of fear; but of power, and of love, and of a sound mind."

Many examples in Scripture show us that God changes names from what people were to what He has made them. He changed Abram (exalted father) to Abraham (father of a multitude), fulfilling the promise to make him a father of many nations; Sarai (princess) to Sarah (mother of nations), and Simon (God has heard) to Peter (Rock). God gave each one a new name, and I believe He does this to show us His power and ability to take something that is broken, weak and frail, and change it into something strong to be used by Him.

When Cindy spoke that night in front of a crowded room, it reminded me that God created us in His image; not the image the world tries to label us with. She is a great example of God's healing power and proof that God took away a label the world gave her, and He replaced it with His own. We are created in the image of our God and we are "fearfully, and wonderfully made!"

Father, we thank You and praise You that You have the power to change what we were, to what you want us to be. Help us push out of our minds, what the world would have us believe, and replace it with Your truth and who You say we are. Amen!

ADDITIONAL READING

John 15:15   Proverbs 22:1   2 Corinthians 5:17

Day 8: Questions to Ponder

1) What nickname or label has been placed on you by others?

2) Have you ever "labeled" others based on what you thought they were like?

3) God wants to change us from being weak spiritually, to being strong in Him. What area in your life do you need God to strengthen?

Day 8 Journal Notes

Day 9
Patience

Be patient therefore, brothers, until the coming of the Lord. Behold, the farmer waits for the precious fruit of the earth, being patient over it, until it receives the early and late rain. James 5:7(WEB)

It was Saturday morning and garage sales were the theme for the day. It's something I like to do, and something my nephew looks forward to doing. I picked him up and we set off on our adventure. His focus was on a specific toy, a Nerf gun. With dollars in his pocket, he was ready! We arrived at the destination and there it was, an RS5 Nerf gun! It was the item he had been looking for! As he headed toward the toy gun of his dreams, another young boy ran up to it first. He carefully examined every inch of it. My nephew stood on the sidelines, just waiting for his turn. Five long minutes passed by, and my nephew was still waiting…. eyes focused on the toy…. never loosing hope and patiently waiting and waiting and still waiting. As I stood back watching him, I wondered if I was like that when it comes to praying and waiting on God to answer my prayers? Did I wait patiently, hopeful that He would answer my prayers?

In the book of James, an example is given of a farmer waiting patiently for his land to yield its crops. In the Middle East, the most important rain would occur twice a year, once in autumn and again in spring. In autumn, it would be to soften and prepare the land for seed and in spring to grow and ripen the crops for harvest. Farmers know that crops will not appear overnight, but that they must wait patiently for them. While the farmer is waiting, they care for the crop, knowing that in due season, they will reap a harvest.

All of us, at one time or another in life, get discouraged and impatient while waiting on God to answer our prayer. But patience is one of the fruits of the Spirit. If we are never put into situations where we can practice patience, then we would never learn to grow in it. So, I encourage you while you are waiting on God to answer your prayer of finding a job, a husband, a wife, healing of a sickness, or a new business adventure, practice being patient. Know that God hears you and that He wants the very best for you. As for my nephew, Ben, his patience paid off. That Nerf gun was tossed aside by that other boy and Ben was waiting patiently on the side lines to pick it up!

Heavenly Father, help us to be patient in all things as we wait on You. Remind us of Your Word as we face day to day trials and encourage us to wait patiently on you! Amen!

ADDITIONAL READING

Proverbs 25:15   **Psalm 40:1**   **Galatians 5:22-23**

Day 9: Questions to Ponder

1) Do you view yourself as a patient person when waiting for something?

2) Have you ever become discouraged while waiting on God to answer your prayer?

3) What are you praying for that is challenging you to be patient?

Day 9 Journal Notes

Day 10
Path of Righteousness

Your word is a lamp to my feet, and a light for my path.
Psalm 119:105(WEB)

A few weeks ago, I stopped by my aunts' house where I was greeted by two friendly dogs. She had just adopted two beautiful dogs. When they approached me, they did this strange thing: they began pushing me in a direction I did not want to go. With their bodies, they pushed against my legs as if to say "Hey, you're headed in the wrong direction." When I asked my aunt what they were doing, she said: "They are herding you." "Huh"? Am I a cow that I should be herded? She told me they were Australian Shepherds and the previous owners had used them to herd horses. She explained that herding dogs were trained to go in front of the animals, to stop or turn the movement of the livestock, either to keep them from danger or to lead them down the right path.

Unfortunately, our human nature tends to do what it wants, whenever it wants to. When we as Christians, go off in a wrong direction or leave the path of righteousness that God has planned for us, I believe God uses things or people to stop or turn our movement and bring us back on course. He gently, by His Holy Spirit, "herds" us in the direction we should be going. He does this to keep us from danger because He wants the very best for our lives. In Numbers 22, God used a donkey to herd Balaam in the right direction. God had given Balaam specific instructions, but Balaam decided to do his own thing. The Bible tells us that God placed an angel with a sword in the middle of the road ready to kill Balaam if he continued traveling the path he was on. It was only when the donkey began to speak that Balaam realized he was heading in the wrong direction. What an eye-opening moment it must have been for Balaam to hear a donkey talk. I bet that event gave Balaam something to talk about around the campfire that night!

Psalm 119 reminds us that God has given us His Word to light our path and lead us in the direction He has planned for us. We can be confident in knowing that when we come to a fork in the road, whether it is to pursue a dating relationship, or to make a career change, or whatever the case may be, if we apply His Word, and seek His will, He will lead us in the direction we should be going.

Heavenly Father, we thank You for Your Word and we ask that You guide us, and You lead us onto the path you have for our lives. Help us to choose the path of righteousness in all we do. Amen!

ADDITIONAL READING

Proverbs 4:11   **Proverbs 3:6**   **Psalm 23:3**

Day 10: Questions to Ponder

1) Have you ever been faced with an important decision and not known which road to take?

2) Sometimes as Christians, we leave the "path of righteousness". Have you ever left the path God called you to walk?

3) Could God be "herding" you in a new direction in life?

Day 10 Journal Notes

Day 11
Ordinary Lives

But God hath chosen the foolish things of the world to confound the wise; and God hath chosen the weak things of the world to confound the things which are mighty; 1Corinthians 1:27(KJV)

Watching the potter begin his work with just an ordinary ball of clay, I couldn't help but think about what the finished product would look like. A lump of clay in my hands would remain just that, an ordinary lump of clay, however, a ball of clay in this potter's hand would turn into something useful, amazing, and unique. It would be something much more than I could ever imagine it would be. As the potter completed his work, the finished product was a beautiful vase. It was now useful. It would be used to display God's artwork, such as beautiful flowers for all to see and enjoy.

Our lives are like that lump of clay. We may see it as something ordinary, or useless. But I believe God looks for those "ordinary" lives in order to display His greatness, His power, and His love.

Gideon, an ordinary man, was chosen by God to deliver Israel out of the hands of their enemy, the Midianites. One day an angel of the Lord appeared to Gideon and calls Gideon a "man of valor" better known as a Mighty Warrior. The angel tells Gideon to go and save Israel from the hands of the Midianites. Gideon, knowing full well that he is not qualified, questions his own ability to save his people and responds to the angel of the Lord telling him that he is the "least" in his father's house. (Judges 6:15) The angel of the Lord assures Gideon that God would be with him. Though Gideon saw himself as the weakest link, God saw something else. You see, Gideon's name means "Destroyer" or "Mighty Warrior". It certainly was not what he was feeling at the moment, nor could he see past his fear. Our feelings can at times, dictate how we respond to certain life issues, but with the power of the Holy Spirit, we can do anything God calls us to do through Christ who is our source of strength. God takes what we see as our weakest area, and turns it around for good, using it for His glory on display for all to see. God took what was an ordinary life which Gideon viewed as the least in his family and used it to save a nation!

Do you view your life as "ordinary"? Are you the weakest in your family? Like that ordinary lump of clay I saw given to the potter that was turned into a beautiful vessel to be used for something extra-ordinary, so can an ordinary life be used for God's glory to do amazing things once it is surrendered to Him.

Father, we offer You our ordinary lives. We ask that You change us and use us as Your vessels to display your greatness. Help us to surrender those weak areas that keep us captive and may you turn them into something strong to be used by You. Amen!

ADDITIONAL READING

Philippians 4:13   **Isaiah 40:29**   **Habakkuk 3:19**

Day 11: Questions to Ponder

1) What area of your life do you feel you are weakest?

2) What gift or talent do you hold that you feel is just ordinary?

3) Is there a part of your life that you need to surrender to the potter so He can make it extra-ordinary?

Day 11 Journal Notes

Day 12
Outward Appearance

But the Lord said unto Samuel, Look not on his countenance, or on the height of his stature; because I have refused him: for the Lord seeth not as man seeth; for man looketh on the outward appearance, but the Lord looketh on the heart. 1 Samuel 16:7(KJV)

Car hunting can be a difficult task, especially, when you have such a tight budget. Last week I purchased a used vehicle. The body was straight, the paint was nice and shiny, the inspection report from the dealer showed the vehicle in good condition, and it matched my budget. "Perfect fit" I thought and so I bought it. The next day, I took it to a mechanic for a quick check to see if any maintenance was needed. His findings were the opposite of what I thought I was getting. Though the outward appearance of the vehicle looked almost new, the heart of the vehicle, the engine, was not good. It needed a new engine.

Samuel, one of the Judges of Israel, was sent by the Lord to seek out a new king who would rule over Israel. (1 Samuel). When Samuel arrived at his destination which was the house of Jesse, he saw the first of Jesse's sons, and judging from his appearance, he thought that this son would be a good fit. However, Samuel is reminded by the Lord, that though man looks on the outward appearance, but the Lord looks at the heart. Samuel quickly learns that this first son was not the one the Lord would have as the new king. Samuel continues down the line, from oldest to youngest, meeting all of Jesse's sons. Finally, he meets the last one the youngest one, who was tending sheep and his name was David. It is then that the Lord confirms that David is to be anointed as the new king. Had Samuel made the selection based ONLY on appearance, what a blessing Israel would have missed.

God looks at our hearts, our motives, our inward thoughts and knows the real us. Even when others judge us from the outside appearance, we can be comforted in knowing that God sees our hearts and motives. May we strive each day to become more like Him.

As for the car I purchased based on the appearance, it turned out to be a lemon. I took it back to the dealer who kindly refunded my money after showing him the mechanics report. The next vehicle I purchase, I will be sure it is not based just on appearance!

Father, help us to be more like You. Remind us that it is You who sees our hearts. Help us not to judge on outward appearances. Amen!

ADDITIONAL READING

Psalm 139:2   **Hebrews 4:12**   **Jeremiah 17:10**

Day 12: Questions to Ponder

1) Have you ever purchased an item based on looks alone without knowing the quality of the item?

2) Do you ever judge others based on the way they dress or the vehicle they drive?

3) The Word of God judges the attitudes of the heart. What heart issue or wrong motive do you need God to change?

Day 12 Journal Notes

Day 13
Grace

For by grace are ye saved through faith; and that not of yourselves: it is the gift of God: Ephesians 2:8(KJV)

Grace. What is it? It is God's unmerited favor. Simply put: Getting what we do not deserve.

As a young driver many years ago, I remember receiving my license. The freedom I felt behind the wheel of my 1965 Mustang was powerful. I no longer had to depend on others to take me places I wanted to go. I could go where I wanted, when I wanted, and drive as fast as I wanted; however, freedom and speed come with a price tag. I had a friend with a bumper sticker which read "Faster Than a Speeding Ticket" and that is how I felt behind the wheel of my 1965 Mustang. So, one day I put that bumper sticker to the test. The flashing red lights behind me soon proved the bumper sticker wrong. With no excuse good enough to get out of the ticket, I knew what was coming next. I deserved the ticket. I was speechless when the Officer approached my vehicle. Not because I had nothing to say, but because his words were not what I expected. His words were full of grace. He looked at me through his mirrored sunglasses and said: "I'm letting you off with a verbal warning." I knew I did not deserve a warning; I deserved a ticket. But I gracefully and happily swallowed by pride and accepted his offer. He showed me Grace, something I did not deserve.

Ephesians 2:8 speaks of God's grace. It reminds us that our salvation is based on God's Grace alone. It is not based on our behavior or things we do right. Nothing we could ever do would earn His grace. God's grace is a free gift, given to us with no strings attached, simply because He loves us. He desires to see us become more like Him. It is by the Grace of God we are changed. God does not leave us in the state He finds us. By His Grace, He changes us; I am not what I use to be, and my past does not define me; Rather, it is by the Grace of God that He is continually changing me into His image, to become more like Him. God's Grace – What a beautiful gift!

Heavenly Father, thank You for Your Grace in our lives. As You have shown us Grace, may we show grace to others in our lives. AMEN!

ADDITIONAL READING

James 4:6   **Titus 2:11**   **Romans 3:24**

Day 13: Questions to Ponder

1) Can you think of a time in your life where someone has showed you grace?

2) Have you ever showed grace to someone who wronged you?

3) God's grace is a free gift. Who in your life do you need to show God's grace?

Day 13 Journal Notes

Day 14
Plans

A man's heart plans his course, but Yahweh directs his steps.
Proverbs 16:9 (WEB)

The Lord knew, before my feet hit the ground on Sunday morning, how my day would play out. I woke up early to fit in a run before Sunday morning service. My original plan was to complete 6 miles on the street, but instead I decided to change my course to a dirt track. I pulled out of my driveway, onto the street and then WHAM! He came out of nowhere and into my lane. The impact was so great, that it pushed my car back and next to a curb. Thankfully, he was not hurt and I was just a bit sore, stiff and shaken! My car on the other hand was not so lucky. It looked beyond repair. But as my friend reminded me: "Cars can be replaced but people cannot." I am thankful that no serious injury occurred.

I wonder if when Job woke up on the morning his calamity hit, if he knew the Lord already had his day planned out. I'm sure he thought it was going to be just another day of his routine. Instead, his day took quite a turn. In one day, Job receives four messages and with each message, comes another loss. In a matter of one day, Job loses everything, from livestock, to servants, to his children. If that was not enough, Job broke out with sores all over his body, compromising his health. Despite his calamity, Job trusted God. He refused to give in and curse God, even when his wife told him too. (Job 2:9). In the end, Job's life was restored. As a result of trusting God, Job was blessed with twice as much as what he lost.

Our days may not turn out the way we planned, but God has a greater purpose, a greater plan. He is all knowing. The Bible tells us that He knows the number of hairs on our head (Luke 12:7), He knows the number of our days (Job 14:5), and He knows the future (Isaiah 46:10), so He certainly knows why our day did not go the way we planned. The maker of the universe knows exactly why your day did not go as you thought it would. Rest in the peace of knowing that nothing will happen today that God does not already know will happen. He is right there beside you, guiding you through your day.

> *Heavenly Father, help us to trust You, even when our plans fail. Though we don't see the end result right away, we know that Your plan is bigger. Help us to choose to trust You, even when life does not make sense. Amen!*

ADDITIONAL READING

Proverbs 16:3   **Psalm 20:4**   **Jeremiah 29:11**

Day 14: Questions to Ponder

1) When your plans fail or when calamity hits your life, do you blame God or question His love for you?

2) What type of calamity are you facing in life that is making it difficult for you to trust God?

3) Name a time in life when God brought you through a difficult life event.

Day 14 Journal Notes

Day 15
Advocate vs Accuser

My little children, these things write I unto you, that ye sin not. And if any man sin, we have an advocate with the Father, Jesus Christ the righteous: 1 John 2:1(KJV)

My sister received a ticket in the mail for parking a vehicle in a "no parking" zone. The problem was it was not her vehicle that was parked illegally. Somehow the law enforcement officer transposed the license plate number, and the ticket was mailed to her. After numerous requests for City officials to review the case and provide a photo of the violation, her request was granted which, revealed her innocence in the matter. The review confirmed that the City was not able to show the vehicle in violation of the law. In Law Enforcement we call this "Burden of Proof", where the accuser must prove that the defendant is guilty.

In life, we at times fail in our walk with Christ, but we have an advocate who pleads our case for us and is standing by ready to forgive us. His great love covers a multitude of sins. The Bible teaches us that if we sin, and confess our sins, He is faithful and just to forgive us of all our wrongs.   It is key to acknowledge our sins to Christ, not cover them up. Besides, He already knows what we have done wrong so why not confess it? I have a mental image in my head when I mess up. I can see the accuser running to the Father saying: "Did you see what she did? She calls herself a Christian." The Father responds back: "Yes, I saw what she did, and I forgive her. She is my child and I love her"….as He gently picks me up, dusts me off and says "let's keep going". God's love for us is so great, that there is nothing that can separate us from Him.

Like my sister, who's ticket was written off, and the case dropped so Christ writes off our offenses if we humbly ask. His cleansing blood is enough to forgive any sin we have committed. Remember You are

God's child, and you belong to Him. When you realize you have sinned, run towards Christ and not away from Him. God's love is so great, that he removes our sins as far as the east is from the west. When the accuser begins to taunt you, remind him that you belong to Christ.

Father, thank You for taking our place on the cross. Thank You for your great love and mercy. May Your Spirit remind us of who we are in You when the accuser begins to point out our sins. May we run to you in repentance, not run away from You. Amen!

ADDITIONAL READING

1 Timothy 2:5   **John 14:2**   **2 Corinthians 5:21**

Day 15: Questions to Ponder

1) When you sin, do you run to the Father with it or do you try and hide it?

2) Is there a sin you have committed that the accuser continually taunts you with and says God won't forgive you?

3) Do you view God as an advocate or an accuser?

Day 15 Journal Notes

Day 16
Comforting Love

*As one whom his mother comforts, so I will comfort you. You will be
comforted in Jerusalem.. Isaiah 66:13(WEB)*

I watched anxiously, as the doctor began the task of placing a cast
on my daughter's leg. Unfortunately, she had broken a bone. The pain
she was in showed on her face, and the pain I felt watching her in discomfort, brought tears to my eyes. Watching our children endure pain is
pure agony. I wanted to take her pain from her. If I could have taken her
place and endured her pain and discomfort for her, I would have.

Our God cares about every detail of our life. He cares when we
are in emotional, physical, or spiritual pain and He longs to comfort us.
All throughout the scriptures, His words remind us of how much He
cares for us and how He longs to console us. Our grief, pain and tears do
not go unnoticed by God. In Psalm 56, the Bible gives an example of
how even our tears mean something to God. He keeps all our tears in a
bottle, every one of them. It does not matter how big or small our grief is,
whether we caused our own pain by disobedience, or whether someone
else caused our tears, God cares about each tear drop that falls from our
eyes.

During a time when the nation of Israel was rebelling against
God's laws, God sends a prophet to them named Isaiah. Isaiah reminded
the nation how God would heal and comfort them if they would just turn
from their rebellious ways. The Bible described their misery as a tossing
sea that lacked rest and comfort. In exchange for the people leaving their
life of sin, God offered a comfort that would be soothing and tender, end-
ing their misery and pain. Only a loving God who cares about our sorrow
and pain could offer such a loving response.

When you feel alone in your trials, you can be assured that God cares and He wants to ease your pain. He has not abandoned you. He loves you and longs to comfort you. He is waiting for you to call on Him so He can extend His arms of compassion and comfort to you.

Father, when we are hurting and long to be comforted, bring to our minds Your comforting words of scripture. May Your Peace fill our hearts and minds and may we sense Your presence of comfort all around us. Amen!

ADDITIONAL READING

Psalm 119:76   Matthew 5:4   2 Corinthians 1:4

Day 16: Questions to Ponder

1) Have you ever been in so much pain that it was difficult to rest or sleep?

2) When you see others go through painful moments in their life, what do you do to help bring them comfort?

3) God longs to comfort us in our misery even if the pain was a result of our sinful ways. What area of life of life do you want to feel God's comfort?

Day 16 Journal Notes

Day 17
Inevitable Changes

To every thing there is a season, and a time to every purpose under the heaven: Ecclesiastes 3:1(KJV)

Change is difficult for me. I am one of those people that avoid change at all costs. I get use to my environment, become comfortable and want life to remain just as it is. Even though I struggle with change, I hold a strong belief that God uses all things to work together for our good, even those changes that we dislike, are uncomfortable with, or think are a mistake.

A few months ago, I was rear-ended while in a work vehicle which left me with an aching back. After weeks of physical therapy, rehabilitation exercises in the gym, and an MRI, (which revealed the injury) I was told I had to change up my exercise routine. "No running for now" was the first thing out of the doctors' mouth. Yikes! I'm a runner at heart, so this was difficult for me to hear. The same week, my friend who works out with me on a daily basis, had to change up her exercise schedule due to work changes and would not be able to work out with me as often as she normally does. That's two changes in one week. Isn't there a law against that? I'm not willing to give up my workouts completely, and I want to get stronger, so I'm leaving behind what I knew as comfortable and familiar (my life as a runner) and embracing the change into the world of weights and muscle building.

In Genesis chapter 12, we see Abraham's life change. The scriptures tell us that the Lord commanded Abraham to take his family and leave his country. God was telling him it's time for a change. I can imagine Abrahams' expression upon hearing the news that his life was about to change. I'm sure he was comfortable with life just the way it was. Now, however, he was about to leave everything that was familiar and comfortable to him and enter a new environment that he knew nothing about. In obedience, Abraham moved to that new land God was calling him to. He did it in faith. He trusted God. He did not question God nor did he look back. He just went. Abraham believed God's promise that he would be blessed. One of those blessings was a son born to him in his old age. Abraham put God first, and God rewarded him greatly by making him the Father of many nations.

When change comes knocking at your door, don't run from it, embrace it. Know that God is allowing it into your life for a good reason and that reason is usually a great blessing!

Father, when change comes into our life, help us to embrace it in faith knowing that You allowed it and You are working all changes for our good. Amen!

ADDITIONAL READING

Romans 8:28   Isaiah 43:19   Romans 12:2

Day 17: Questions to Ponder

1) Change can be difficult for some people. Do you welcome change or run from it?

2) Have you had to make a recent change in your life that you find is difficult?

3) What is God showing you about your life that he wants to change?

Day 17 Journal Notes

Day 18
Exchanging Fear for Faith

Anxiety in a man's heart weighs it down, but a kind word makes it glad.
Proverbs 12:25(WEB)

Anxiety, worry, and fear all play a part in stress. Anxiety can come when we least expect it. It creeps up when we are focused on a problem and seem to have no way of solving it. I struggle with anxiety which in turn leads to stress. When I get stressed, I do goofy things. A few years ago I became stressed at work due to unforeseen events, so in an attempt to de-stress, I decided to take a few days off. The first day of my vacation I woke up thinking I was late for work. After realizing I was on vacation, I stumbled to the kitchen for a bowl of cereal. Not fully awake, I reached for the Almond milk and began pouring it on my cereal but something about the taste of the cereal just didn't seem right. It was salty. I looked down at the carton to check the date and discovered it was the carton of chicken broth I had poured on my cereal not Almond milk. Anxiety and stress can make you do crazy things!

I am convinced that God does not want us to be anxious, to worry, or to fear about any problem life may bring us. Jesus spoke about this when he told his disciples not to be anxious about life. As a matter of fact, Jesus uses the example of birds when referring to worry. He reminds us that if He cares for the birds (who cannot plant or store up food for themselves) then we who are worth much more, will also be taken of. He also reminds us that we cannot change our circumstances by worrying.

Often, we fret or despair over difficulties that we encounter daily; however, God already knows our struggle and He knows the anxiety we have in our hearts. He does not want us to be anxious; on the contrary, He wants us to have faith in Him to deliver us from that problem. His word tells us that He has not given us a spirit of fear but rather a sound mind. One of the tools God has given us to combat those fears is the Word of God. When those fears begin to come up in your mind, the spiritual battle begins. Use the scripture to fight against those fears. When you think you are alone in the struggle, remember the Word of God says He will never leave or forsake you. When you think your needs won't be met, God's Word says that He will provide. When you think you cannot accomplish a job task, Philippians 4 says that you can do all things through Christ.

What are you anxious over today? What fear are you facing? What are you worried about? There is no difficulty that God cannot deliver you from. Seek God and He will deliver you from all your fears!

Father God, as we call out to You to deliver us from our fear, we know You hear us. Help us to bring our anxious thoughts, fears, and worries and lay them at Your feet. Comfort our hearts with Your peace and help us exchange our fears for faith in You. Amen!

ADDITIONAL READING

2 Timothy 1:7   **Matthew 6:34**   **1 Peter 5:7**

Day 18: Questions to Ponder

1) What causes you to worry, fear, or to become anxious?

2) When you begin to worry or become fearful, do you seek God in prayer?

3) The Bible tells us to cast our cares on God because he cares or us. What anxious thoughts or fears do you want to hand over to God?

Day 18 Journal Notes

Celebrations of Life

And God is able to make all grace abound to you, that you, always hav-
ing all sufficiency in everything, may abound to every good work.
2 Corinthians 9:8(WEB)

With the house beautifully decorated with happy birthday signs, we waited with anticipation for our friend Cyndi to arrive home. It was her birthday, the big 5-0 and we were ready to celebrate it with a surprise party for her. Unsure of when she would arrive home, we all waited with excitement for her arrival. We knew she would be there, but not sure of the time she would arrive. We tried to remain quiet so we could hear the garage door open since this would be our confirmation that she was home, but with several women in one room chatting about the latest life events, that was a challenge. And then finally we heard it. The garage door opened, and we knew she was home! As she walked through the door we all yelled out SURPRISE! Surprised she was! The expression on her face was well worth the time spent waiting for her. (Though I think we shouted a bit too loud because it left her with a splitting headache). She knew she was loved and appreciated by those surrounding her with gifts and hugs, to celebrate her special day!

The Bible is filled with celebrations. In the Parable of the Lost Coin, found in Luke 15, we read about a woman who had ten coins and lost one. She searches the house, looking in every corner and when she finds it, she calls her friends to come celebrate with her. That is the kind of celebration God's angels have every time one lost soul turns to God. It is a true celebration of life!

God longs to spend time with us and to share in every part of our life. Just like when we waited for Cyndi to arrive home so we could shower her with gifts and celebrate her birthday, so God waits for us to invite Him into our lives so He can shower us with His gifts. The Bible describes God's gifts as the perfect gift coming down from above. Nothing the world can offer can ever measure up to the good things God has for us. He is waiting patiently for us to invite him into every area of our life. Is there an area of your life that you are keeping from God? Regardless of what area it is, He loves you and he is waiting there patiently for you to invite Him into all areas of your life to shower you with His blessings!

Heavenly Father, thank You for Your wonderful gift of salvation which You have freely offered to us. We invite You into our lives. Help us to let go and surrender all areas of our life into Your hands. May You bless us with ever good and perfect gift from above. Amen!

ADDITIONAL READING

James 1:17   **Romans 11:29**   **Ecclesiastes 3:13**

Day 19: Questions to Ponder

1) What was your all-time favorite birthday, Christmas, or other gift you received?

2) When we invite Christ into our life He gives us the ultimate gift of eternal life. Have you invited Christ into your life?

3) Is there any area in your life that you have not surrendered to Christ?

Day 19 Journal Notes

Day 20
Prayer Changes Things

"

Then they cry to Yahweh in their trouble, and he brings them out of their distress. Psalm 107:28(WEB)

Located in Riverside, CA, is a large orange billboard sign which reads in bold letters: PRAYER CHANGES THINGS. That sign was placed along a busy street where hundreds of cars pass by every day. It is a constant reminder to those that see it, that prayer does change circumstances. I believe kneeling in prayer to our Father in Heaven can change any circumstance and bring a great movement of God.

Recently my mother along with others, have been praying for her health condition. She struggles with pulmonary fibrosis, which attacks the lungs. She uses an oxygen unit to help her breath easier. The portable tanks she uses when she is away from home are difficult for her to carry so we started searching for a different unit. We found one, that was much lighter to carry, but unfortunately the insurance company refused to pay for it. The cost to purchase it on our own was close to $3,000 and our budget could not cover the expenses. We brought it to our heavenly Father in prayer. We continued to pray that God would provide either the finances to cover it or for the unit to be approved by the insurance company. During her doctor visit this week, she again requested a lighter unit, and the doctor once again put in the request to the insurance company. Before the day was over, the insurance company had agreed to pay for it. The very next day, my mama had her new oxygen unit. Prayer answered!

In 1 Kings, 17 we read of the prophet Elijah visiting a woman whose son had just died of an illness. Elijah takes the boy from his mothers' arms and prayed for God to restore life back into the boy. The Bible tells us that Elijah stretched himself over the boy three times and cried out to God for healing. The Lord heard Elijah's cry and restored life back into the boy. What a wonderful example of the power of prayer!

What are you praying for? Is it salvation for a son or daughter that has walked away from the faith? Is it for financial freedom from debt? Or is it simply to know God on a deeper level? Keep praying. Don't give up. God has not forgotten you. God hears your prayers, and He loves you. Keep praying!

Father, You are all powerful and we know You hear our prayers. Help us to not lose faith in You when our answer to prayer does not come immediately. Give us strength to keep praying and to keep seeking You. Amen!

ADDITIONAL READING

Psalm 6:9   Isaiah 65:24   1 Thessalonians 5:17

Day 20: Questions to Ponder

1) How often do you reach out to God through prayer?

2) Do you become discouraged when your prayers are not answered immediately?

3) God always hears our prayers. The Bible teaches us to never stop praying. Who or what are you praying for?

Day 20 Journal Notes

_____

_____

_____

_____

_____

_____

_____

_____

_____

_____

_____

_____

_____

_____

_____

Day 21
Choosing to Forget

I, even I, am he who blots out your transgressions for my own sake; and I
will not remember your sins. *Isaiah 43:25(WEB)*

I woke up groggy not knowing where I was. Everything was in a
fog. I tried to get up, but my legs would not cooperate. So, there I lay,
until the anesthesia wore off. The nurse assured me that the fog would
soon pass, and I would be up on my feet in no time. Sometimes the
things we say while coming off the anesthesia can be quite embarrassing.
My daughter and my friend were both with me, reminding me of the
goofy things I said. I'm glad I don't remember what I said but somehow,
I think they will not let me forget.

In Isaiah 43 we are reminded of God's love for us and His forgiv-
ing power. He reminds us that what He forgives, He chooses to forget.
The Bible says that God can blot out our sins. If you take a pen and blot
out a word, the ink will cover up what was written before making it as
though it was never there. When I think of blotting something out, it is as
if it never occurred. Like a prisoner who has been exonerated for their
crimes and set free from prison, so it is when God blots our sins. They
are covered up, stained over by the blood of the Lamb. We are pardoned
from our sins and God has chosen to forget them. They are erased, dis-
solved, expunged.

Our God never forgets us, He only forgets our sins which is by
His choice. His decision to not remember our sins, is deliberate, a con-
scious effort. Our human nature finds it difficult to forgive others when
they sin against us, and we may never forget the wrong done to us even
when we do forgive them. However, our God is ready and waiting to forgive and forget our transgressions if we just ask.

Knowing that God forgives our sins when we ask, shows me His great love for us. But knowing that he CHOOSES to not remember our sins, shows me His Amazing Grace!

Father, thank You for your great love for us and the forgiveness You so freely offer to us. May You remind us to forgive others who wrong us, just as You have forgiven us from all our sins. Amen!

ADDITIONAL READING

1 John 1:9　　**Isaiah 44:22**　　**Psalm 103:12**

Day 21: Questions to Ponder

1) Name an embarrassing moment or event you would rather forget.

2) Do you find it difficult to forgive and forget when others offend you?

3) When we confess our sins to God, He forgives us. What unconfessed sin do you want God to forgive?

Day 21 Journal Notes

Day 22
Hurting Heart

Lord, all my desire is before You. My groaning is not hidden from You.
Psalm 38:9(WEB)

God knows what we need before we even ask. He knows our hearts and He knows when we are hurting. Even if we choose to keep our hurts to ourselves, God knows our pain. Nothing is hidden from His eyes. In those times of our deepest longing for comfort, The Lord may choose to send a friend our way to let us know He hears us. It could be the checker at the market or the barista at the coffee counter. He uses each of us, to strengthen one another. Our words of encouragement to a hurting heart often bring comfort to the one receiving them, and a blessing to the one speaking to them.

I received a call from a friend who said he had a God moment. His name is Jason and he has allowed me to tell his story. He told me he stayed home from work because he was depressed. He was going through a divorce and the pain he was feeling seemed unbearable. He said had prayed but felt like God was not listening. Feeling overwhelmed by his circumstances and feeling like a failure in life, he wanted to give up. In the late morning, he received a knock on his door. It was a city worker who came by to trim his backyard trees which were overgrown into the telephone wires. Annoyed, Jason let him in. The city worker chuckled at Jason's Snoopy P.J.'s, which sparked a conversation. Jason began to share his broken heart with the city worker. He explained that he was depressed, did not want to go on in life, and had no hope for a future. The City worker began to share his faith with Jason, reminding him that God knew his pain, and that God had a future for him. Jason's face brightened, knowing that God had heard his silent prayer and seen the pain in his heart. It changed Jason's outlook on life that day all because the tree trimmer spoke the Lord's words of encouragement!

When your heart is overwhelmed with grief, sorrow, or pain, remember that the Lord sees you. Nothing is hidden from His sight. He is all knowing, all powerful, and cares for you. He is a God who longs to bring you comfort, healing, and love.

Heavenly Father, help us be sensitive to Your leading and that when we see those who are downcast, that we would remind them of Your words of comfort. May we be Your vessel to offer hope to a hurting world. Amen!

ADDITIONAL READING

Proverbs 15:3   **Psalm 56:8**   **Psalm 34:15**

Day 22: Questions to Ponder

1) Name a time you experienced pain or felt overwhelmed by life and questioned if God knew your pain.

2) Has anyone ever reminded you that God cares when you were going through a difficult time?   Do you remind others of God's Love when you see them hurting?

3) The Bible tells us that God keeps track of all our sorrows. What painful area of your life do you want God to bring His healing comfort to?

Day 22 Journal Notes

Day 23
Trusting Through Darkness

When I am afraid, I will put my trust in you. Psalm 56:3(WEB)

I spent some time yesterday visiting a Christian friend who is passing away from cancer. She doesn't know when her last day on this earth will be, though she had asked God to tell her. As she began to read from her daily devotion book, the daily reading was about heaven. Through the words on the page, God spoke directly to her heart, gently reminding her that only He knew the day when she would reach her destination to Heaven---not one day early, and not one day too late.   It was like the devotion was written just for her for this day in time!

Trusting in the Lord is not always easy, especially in dark times such as sickness and death. When life spins out of our control and when we are unable to change our circumstances, we fear and begin to question if God really cares. I believe the Lord can use these painful, dark times to stretch our faith and teach us to trust in Him. In Psalm 56:3, King David admits his fear when he says these words: "When I am afraid, I will put my trust in You".

In 2 Chronicles 20, the Bible tells us a story of the people of Judah who were about to enter a battle with their enemies. Feeling overwhelmed and knowing they were outnumbered 3-1, their king Jehoshaphat led them in prayer. During the prayer, the Spirit of the Lord came upon one of the men standing there. His name was Jahaziel (the name means that God sees). Jahaziel speaks hope and tells them not to be afraid for the battle belongs to God. He continues to tell them that they will not need to fight, rather they would just stand there and watch the Lord's victory. The battle ends with Judah watching as their enemies turned on each other. Not one enemy of Judah was left alive. All of Judah praised God that day for watching over them, and for the victory He had given them.

God knows the outcome of your battle. He may choose not to give you the whole picture or the exact day your battle will end, but He does give His promise to never leave us or forsake us. God sees you and is watching over you. He is right there next to you, gently guiding you to the next step.

Father God, remind us that You are right here next to us, leading us through the darkness. As we continue on in our battle, may we not forget that You will NEVER leave us or forsake us. Help us to not be afraid and help us to place our trust in only You. Amen!

ADDITIONAL READING

Joshua 1:9   **Isaiah 41:10**   **Psalm 23:4**

Day 23: Questions to Ponder

1) Trusting God in dark times can be difficult, especially when we don't know what the end result will be. What recent life event has you afraid to trust God?

2) God promises to never leave us or forsake us. Have you ever felt alone when facing a battle?

3) What battle do you need to place in God's hands and rely on Him to bring you through it?

Day 23 Journal Notes

Day 24
Talents

Having then gifts differing according to the grace that is given to us, whether prophecy, let us prophesy according to the proportion of faith; Romans 12:6(KJV)

God has given each of us a talent. They differ from person to person. It may be music, encouragement, or teaching to name a few. I have watched others use a talent or gift the Lord has given them. It started as a desire in their heart. Once they began to exercise it, put it into practice, and nurture it, it grew into something spectacular. Your talent is like a muscle. The more you use it, the stronger it gets. When the Lord provides an open door for the talent He has given you, step up and use it to serve the body of Christ and watch it grow. Others will be blessed by your simple act of obedience!

A parable is told of a man who was leaving on a trip and he left his possessions with three of his servants. To the first servant the master gave three talents, (a talent was said to have been valued at several years of wages), to the second servant he gave two talents, and to the third servant he gave one talent. After entrusting his possessions with his servants, the master left on his journey. The first two servants invested their money wisely and doubled the master's talents, but the third servant did nothing with his money except to bury it in the ground. When the master of the house returned from his journey, he called on each servant to find out what they did with the money given them. The first two servants reported they had doubled their investments and the master was pleased and rewarded them; however, upon hearing that the third servant did nothing with the money given him, the master of the house was furious and takes back what little he had entrusted to the third servant. The master tells him he could have placed the money in the bank where it would have gained at least some interest. No reward was given to the third servant; instead, the master called him lazy and banished him from his house.

God has given each one of us a talent to be used for His good. One of the reasons God gives those talents is to bless the body of believers and to encourage each other. I encourage you today, whatever gifts and talents the Lord has entrusted you with, to look for opportunities where it can be used for the Glory of God. Remember, the more you use your talent, the stronger it will get!

Father, thank you for gifts You have entrusted to us. I ask that You give us boldness, strength, and opportunity to use them to bring glory to Your name. Amen!

ADDITIONAL READING

1 Peter 4:10   1 Corinthians 12:4   1 Corinthians 12:7

Day 24: Questions to Ponder

1) What talent or gift do you hold? Do you play an instrument, sing, write, encourage others?

2) Romans 12:6-8 describes some of the gifts God has given us. Which gift do you believe you have?

3) Like a muscle that grows stronger as you exercise it, so our gifts and talents grow stronger as we use them for the glory God. What gift or talent would you like God to help you get stronger at?

Day 24 Journal Notes

Day 25
Your Keeper

The Lord shall preserve thee from all evil: he shall preserve thy soul.
Psalm 121:7(KJV)

Do you remember the team building exercise you played when you were a kid? It was called "Trust Fall" in which you would close your eyes and fall back into the arms of the one that was supposed to catch you. You would have to rely on your teammate, trusting them with everything within you, that they would catch you as you fell backwards. The idea of putting that type of trust in anyone would require strong faith. To be honest, it probably would take me a lifetime to build up strong faith for that type of exercise!

My niece experienced a similar event when she went to science camp last week. She shared with me that her group had an opportunity to try "Belaying". I did not know what Belaying was, so she educated me. She explained that she climbed up a 100-foot tree, and supported only by a rope, she jumped off. She said she was not afraid because she knew the rope was secure and that it would keep her from harm should she start to fall. Not sure I would try this, but I will make sure I am there next time to cheer her on!

In Psalm 121 the Psalmist reminds us that the Lord will keep us from all harm and will watch over our lives. Like a life preserver used to keep someone safe from drowning, God can keep us safe from the evil around us. Peter, the disciple of Jesus, knew this. The Bible tells us that Peter got out of the boat when Jesus called for him and began to walk on water towards the Lord. What an amazing sight to see! But then Peter began to focus more on the howling wind around him and doubt filled his mind. He began to fear and started to sink. He shouts out to the Lord to save him, and Jesus reached out his had and caught him.

We can trust in the Lord to protect us regardless of the trial we are in. Whether our finances are attacked, we are facing a layoff, or the doctor report does not look good, remember that we can place our trust in the Savior. He will be there to catch us as we fall back into His loving arms!

Father God, as we place all our cares into your hands, may you build within us a strong faith in You. Remind us that you will catch us if we begin to fall. We choose to place our trust in you. Amen!

ADDITIONAL READING

Psalm 32:7   **Isaiah 43:2**   **2 Thessalonians 3:3**

Day 25: Questions to Ponder

1) Name a time when you had to rely on others to help you get through a difficult situation?

2) Is it difficult for you to place your trust in God when you are up against a struggle in life?

3) In Isaiah 43:2 God tells us He will be with us through our difficulty. What difficulty are you facing that is causing you to rely on God to keep you safe?

Day 25 Journal Notes

Day 26
On High Alert

Be sober and self-controlled. Be watchful. Your adversary, the devil,
walks around like a roaring lion, seeking whom he may devour.
1 Peter 5:8(WEB)

They rushed me---there were three of them and I was outnumbered! No chance to outrun them because I did not even see them coming until…. CHOMP! It was too late. I let out a loud OUCH! I had just been bit by a large dog. It happened when a neighbor down the street opened his door and having lost control of his dogs, the three of them rushed out to see who this stranger was knocking on their door. The greeting I received from them was less than friendly---quite rude to be exact. However, they were doing their job which was protecting their property. They were alert and watchful. Ready to protect their home from any stranger that may invade their home. Maybe if I'd been a bit more alert, I could have avoided the CHOMP I received.

In 1 Peter 5:8, we are reminded to be alert and watchful, in order to guard against the enemy of this world who seeks to destroy our faith in Christ. The Bible describes this enemy as one who roams around seeking someone to devour. His purpose is to kill, steal, and destroy life which is the opposite of God's purpose for our lives. Jesus comes to give life so that we may live life more abundantly. He has our best interest in mind and wants us to live life to the fullest, complete, lacking nothing.

By staying in the Word daily and meditating on it, we begin to recognize when the enemy is attacking us. An attack could come in the form of a temptation to sin against God. It could be an attack of the mind where we doubt God's Word, question His existence, or think that He does not care about our sufferings. Through the power of the Holy Spirit, we are given wisdom to know what to do during these attacks. Our

God is more powerful and wiser than any scheme the enemy may be trying to plot against us. As you go through this life remember, stay alert, stay in the Word, and be watchful. It just might help you avoid getting "chomped".

Father, I ask that You help us stay alert and watchful. Help us resist temptation when it comes our way. Give us wisdom to know Your voice in EVERY situation. Amen!

ADDITIONAL READING

Colossians 4:2   Matthew 24:42   1 Corinthians 16:13

Day 26: Questions to Ponder

1) Describe a time when you felt your faith was under attack.

2) The Bible tells us to stay alert and be watchful because the enemy seeks to destroy our lives. How do you respond when the enemy begins to attack your mind with lies?

3) We are told in Mark 14:38 to watch and pray so that we may not enter into temptation. Is there an area of your life where you need to be more watchful over and pray more about?

Day 26 Journal Notes

Day 27
Mustard Seed of Faith

The Lord said, "If you had faith like a grain of mustard seed, you would tell this sycamore tree, 'Be uprooted, and be planted in the sea,' and it would obey you. Luke 17:6(WEB)

I stared at the packet filled with tiny specks, wondering what they were. "They are mustard seeds" my mother pointed out, "plant them, and you can have a mustard tree". They were extremely small and had there not been several in the package, the eye would have missed it. If I could compare them in size to something, it would be as small as a grain of sand. In fact, they are so small, that one would need Faith to believe that anything would actually grow from these tiny little specks. Though mustard seeds are the smallest of all seeds, when planted they can grow up to 20 feet tall, that is if you have enough faith to plant the seed! So, I decided to put my Faith into action, and I planted the seeds. A few days later I began to see the results of my faith: the mustard seeds began to sprout!

The Bible describes faith as having the assurance that what we hope for will come about even though we cannot yet see it. Simply put, faith is believing without seeing proof ahead of time.

Scripture tells the story of a man named Naaman, which is found in 2 Kings. Naaman was a commander of a large army. Stricken with leprosy and seeking healing, he goes out to see Elisha the prophet of God. Elisha sends two servants to give Naaman simple instructions of washing in the Jordon River seven times to receive his healing. Thinking it was a ridiculous request, Naaman storms away. I suppose his idea of healing was something more radical than just dipping in a muddy river. After all who does that, and besides, that would require faith. The two servants go after Naaman and convince him of the error of his ways, and at that moment, Naaman, by faith, believing that he would receive healing, goes and dips in the muddy river. It is then, after complying with what he thought was a ridiculous request, that he is healed. Naaman's faith, plus his action, resulted in healing.

We all have faith in something. Your faith will either lead you towards God or away from Him. The Bible teaches us that we must have faith in God for without faith, we cannot please Him. What are you placing your faith in? Is it based on the size of your bank account? Is it your employer? Someone other than God? Place your faith in God who promises to take care of you. Remember, it doesn't take much faith, just a tiny mustard seed of faith.

Heavenly Father, I pray that you would provide us that small amount of faith we need to trust You. As we place our faith in You, help us to grow stronger in our relationship with you. Amen!

ADDITIONAL READING

Hebrews 11:6   Romans 10:17   2 Corinthians 5:7

Day 27: Questions to Ponder

1) What is your definition of faith?

2) Faith has been described as believing without seeing proof ahead of time. Do you have that kind of faith?

3) The Bible says that without faith it is impossible to please God. Do you have faith in God or have you placed your faith in another source?

Day 27 Journal Notes

Day 28
Mood Makeover

But don't forget to be doing good and sharing, for with such sacrifices
God is well pleased. Hebrews 13:16(WEB)

I struggled to get out of bed the other morning. The mood I was in was less than pleasant and I'm sure others around me would have preferred I took a day off from life. The stressfulness of the week was adding up and I was finding it difficult to praise God even in the little things. Besides, giving praise in the midst of my difficult circumstances would be a sacrifice, something I didn't want do. Later that evening I had been scheduled to lead worship for a small group. I tried to shake the mood off before I arrived, but it wouldn't budge. Still, I was committed to leading worship and so my mood came along for the ride. After music practice, I stepped outside, called two friends and shared my struggle. They prayed for me to get through the evening. As I began worship that evening, my burden began to lift and my mood brightened. I guess you could say I had a Mood Makeover!

A sacrifice is giving up something for the benefit of another, even if it is painful or unpleasant. It is an act of love. Giving praise to God, even in our unpleasant moods can be a painful sacrifice, and I suppose it is why the Bible calls it a "Sacrifice of Praise". But, praising God in the midst of your pain has its' benefits. King David, spoken of in the book of Psalm must have known the benefit of a sacrifice of praise to God. In Psalm 119 it says he praised God seven times a day and I'm sure King David didn't always have the best of days; Yet, the Bible tells us that he continually gave praise to God. David was a musician, so it is easy for me to identify with him when it comes to singing praise. It is a blessing to offer my gifts and talents over to God to be used by him to edify others in the church who may be struggling. I could have chosen to back out of leading worship based on my feelings, but instead I chose to fulfill a commitment. It was through that sacrifice of praise to the Lord, that my mood had a makeover. It was almost as if God was waiting to see if I would still praise Him, regardless of what I was feeling at the time.

What are you holding onto that is keeping you from offering a sacrifice of praise to God? Is it hurtful words spoken to you by family or friends? Are you disappointed over the job you didn't get? Or is your anxiety and worry so high, it is causing you to lose hope that things will ever get better? Stop, look up, lift your voice, and give a shout of praise to God for things he has already done for you. Praise God even if you don't feel like it because it wouldn't be a sacrifice of praise if it didn't cost you something.

Father God, teach us to continually praise you, even in the unpleasant times of life. Show us the blessings you have in store for us as we offer you our sacrifice of praise. Amen!

ADDITIONAL READING

Psalm 146:2   **Jonah 2:9**   **Psalm 119:164**

Day 28: Questions to Ponder

1) Name something God has done that you can give him praise for.

2) Do you find it difficult to offer God praise when you are going through a trial or when you are in an unpleasant mood?

3) The Bible tells us to offer a sacrifice of praise to God. What are you currently facing that is keeping you from offering up your sacrifice of praise?

Day 28 Journal Notes

Day 29
What Should We Pray

In the same way, the Spirit also helps our weaknesses, for we don't know how to pray as we ought. But the Spirit himself makes intercession for us with groanings which can't be uttered.
Romans 8:26 (WEB)

The text popped up on my cell phone which read "Please pray for me". It was from a family member who had been faced with some recent challenges. Her text left me wondering what was wrong. Since she was not specific, I did not know what to pray for. I paused for a moment then bowed my head and prayed on her behalf, asking God to meet her need and show himself strong in her struggle. Later that day, she called to explain her text. She mentioned having a family crisis at hand and did not know how or what to pray for. The pain she felt inside was so overwhelming, she could not describe it with words. Above all, she wanted God's will to be done, but she did not know what his will was in her crisis.

As believers, we are urged to pray for one another, even intercede on their behalf when needed as described in 1 Timothy. Prayer is our number one source of strength. A Jewish teacher once said: "He who prays, surrounds his house with a wall stronger than iron." I know when I am hurting and unable to pray, I want to be surrounded by others who are praying for me. I want that "wall of iron" surrounding me. Especially in times of life when we are faced with circumstances beyond our control. Some struggles bring so much pain and heartache that we don't know what to do, what to say, or how to pray for God's will. The emotional pain can be so deep that all we have are groans to express our heartache. The apostle Paul sheds some light this subject. Romans 8 teaches us that when we do not know what to pray for, the Spirit steps in and intercedes on our behalf in order to bring about the will of God in our circumstance. Intercession is an act of intervening on behalf of someone, a prayer offered to God on behalf of the other person. We may not know how or what to pray at times, but the Spirit of the Lord searches our hearts and minds and knows exactly what to pray for. When all we can muster up are just groans expressing our pain, the Holy Spirit who intercedes for us translates those groans and offers up a prayer on our behalf to our Heavenly Father who sees, hears, and knows our pain. Rest assured, your groans which are turned into prayers are heard. The Father cares deeply for you and keeps track of all our sorrows. Not one is forgotten.

What pain are you holding on to that is so deep that only groans can express your turmoil? Who is God calling you to intercede for in life? Lift that person in prayer to the Lord and pray for them daily. And if you are the one expressing those groans of pain, know that our Father in heaven hears, knows, and cares!

Father God, as we express our pain through groans, help us to remember that you do care for us, that you know our pain and hear our prayers. Teach us to be sensitive to the leading of your Holy Spirit and faithful in praying for those around us that are hurting. Amen!

ADDITIONAL READING

1 Timothy 2:1   **Hebrews 7:25**   **Ephesians 6:18**

Day 29: Questions to Ponder

1) Have you ever faced a crisis and didn't know what to pray for?

2) Prayer is one of our most valuable tools and can be a source of strength when we are hurting. Do you ask others to pray for you when you are going through a painful experience?

3) The Bible tells us that when we don't know what to pray, the Spirit Himself intercedes for us. What need or painful experience are you having a difficult time expressing to God?

Day 29 Journal Notes

Day 30
Promise Keeper

He has remembered his covenant forever, the word which he commanded
to a thousand generations.
Psalm 105:8(WEB)

"Hey you"! I heard a voice behind me yell out. It was Ray, the elderly man I met several weeks prior at a senior center while making a delivery. Ray had lost his wife a few years ago and to help fill the lonely hours he had begun painting as a hobby. "I forgot your name", he said "but I remembered your painting". Ray may have forgotten my name, but he didn't forget the promise he made to me. His face displayed this glow of satisfaction and he beamed with excitement, proud that he had remembered to bring me this gift he had promised me. "I promised you I would paint a butterfly for you and I always keep my promises" he said. Ray handed me the painting which was a beautiful orange and black butterfly. I could tell he had spent lots of time on it because of the great detail. "I never break my promises" he reminded me again, "I always keep them". Ray was a promise keeper.

Noah was a man that knew God's promises well. Remember him? The ark, the animals, and the flood? His story is found in Genesis 6. The earth was filled with evil and God was displeased. To rid the earth of its corruption, God told Noah that he was going to send a flood to destroy the earth and all that was in it; however, God makes a promise to Noah and tells him that he and his family will be spared. While all others on the earth laughed in disbelief of the thought of a flood coming, Noah chose to take God at His word and built an ark. The rain came, filled the earth, and destroyed all those left outside the ark. The only survivors of the flood were Noah and his family. God promised Noah, that he would never again send a flood to destroy all the earth. (Genesis 9). As a reminder, God places a rainbow (yes, God created the rainbow) in the clouds as a sign of the promise He made to never send a flood to destroy the earth again. God had kept His promise.

All of God's promises are true. He makes no empty promises. God always does what He says He will do. In Psalm 105 we are told that God remembers his promises forever, even for a thousand generations. God placed the rainbow in the sky thousands of years ago, and it can still be seen today after a rainfall. You can trust in God, the Great Promise Keeper!

Father God, we thank you and praise you that you are truth. Every word you speak can be trusted to come to pass. Help us remember your promises in times when we struggle with doubt. Reassure our hearts that your promises are true. Amen!

ADDITIONAL READING

Genesis 9:15   **Numbers 23:19**   **Psalm 105:42**

Day 30: Questions to Ponder

1) Do you always keep your promise?

2) Has someone ever made a promise to you and then didn't keep it?

3) God never breaks His promises to us. Every word He speaks is truth. Do you ever doubt God's word?

Day 30 Journal Notes

Dedication

This book, Upward Path for Spiritual Training, is dedicated to my mother, Sandra Price, who is now with the Lord. Her unconditional love and support have inspired me to write these devotions. The love she has shown me throughout my life, even in the difficult years of my growing up, closely reflects the love God has for us. She taught me the ways of the Lord by serving the Lord with all her heart, mind, and soul. I am blessed to have had her as a mother.

I love you mom!

Acknowledgements

I want to express my deepest gratitude to my Lord and Savior Jesus Christ, who gave me the ability to write these devotions.

My heartfelt appreciation goes to my beloved mother Sandra Price who is now with the Lord. Thank you for being my biggest cheerleader and encourager.

To my daughter, Cassie Price: You give me inspiration to keep writing. I love you!

To my sister Lucy McReynolds and nieces Sarah McReynolds and Samantha Castellanos for their contribution, love and support.

To Verna Hargrove, my writing mentor. Thank you for spending countless hours with me and allowing me to shadow you during this process.

To Cyndi Richau, thank you for always encouraging me to finish this devotional book and never letting me quit. Your friendship is a blessing!

To Shelley Lesley, who suggested I begin journaling in the first place, and who came up with the title for this book based on Proverbs 15:24.

A heartfelt thank you to Lori Soto, and Cindy Searey for your encouragement, and sound advice.

A big thank you to all those who have supported me through this process and for allowing me to tell your story through these devotions.

About the Author

Lori Price is a passionate advocate for physical fitness and spiritual growth. As a mother, musician, and entrepreneur based in Southern California, she draws inspiration from her life experiences and the diverse individuals she has encountered. When she's not crafting devotional writings, she laces up her running shoes, wholeheartedly embracing the joy of running. Additionally, she actively serves her local church, dedicating her time to both volunteering and contributing to the worship team for Celebrate Recovery. Her devotion to physical fitness and spiritual wellness shines through in her heartfelt and transformative writing.

Made in the USA
Las Vegas, NV
06 August 2024

93453713R00075